DROPS OF GOLD

Emma Curtis Hopkins

CONTENTS

January

January 1. How strong your thoughts are! Each one attracts circumstances to you just like itself. Send this thought abroad over the universe and draw unto yourself great possessions, such as it is sure to bring: "I trust in the Principle of Righteousness."

January 2. Your inner nature is fine and brave. The government is on your shoulders; therefore, you should much repeat these words of Jesus Christ: "All power is given unto me, in heaven and in earth."

January 3. You have large ambitions. You can carry out your hidden ideals by spending many night watches affirming: "I am one with Divine Wisdom"

January 4. You are the patron Saint by nature of literature, art, and education. All that you favor prospers if you have learned to spend all vacant moments silently whispering: "I am good."

January 5. You can master the business of the world if you investigate its ways and do not cease from believing: "All things are mine, for God is my Friend."

January 6. Your speech does charm the ears of congregations of men, if you have been faithful to the motto born with you, to be silently spoken day and night: "I am Spirit."

January 7. You have wondrous sympathies, and philanthropy. Carry out your greatness by determining: "I am meek and lowly of heart."

January 8. You will draw revenues and judgment to yourself by saying: "My help cometh from Jehovah."

January 9. Great are your aspirations. Realize them by affirming silently: "God is my Strength and my Life."

January 10. To think and reason wisely is your inheritance. Say these words daily that the world may be benefited by you: "My Mind is God."

January 11. You can work nobly for a cause. Say often: "God works through me to will and to do that which ought to be done by me."

January 12. You will learn your mission in life by saying continually: "God is my Judge."

January 13. You are great of heart and mind by birthright. Demonstrate this by keeping for your life-text: "God is the strength of my Life. Of whom then shall I be afraid!"

January 14. You can prophesy of things to come. Get down on your knees to Jehovah, saying: "Thou knowest all things."

January 15. Positiveness, executiveness, and determination, you have by nature. Say continually: "I know no fear. God is my Friend."

January 16. Nothing can keep you from being at the head of a large and successful enterprise if you have held daily the idea: "God prospers me."

January 17. You expect largely, and great fulfillment belongs to you. Prove these words true by getting the potentiality of this formula: "God is Love. I am Love. God is Power. I am Power."

January 18. You are a natural promoter of harmony and social joy. You have demonstrated this already if you have said often: "God is my Peace."

January 19. You swing your world from right to left according to your dictum. Be sure to enter into sleep nightly with this thought: "Divine Wisdom is demonstrated by the perfect judgment with which I administer upon affairs."

January 20. You are the national financier if for your motto you take: "The earth is the Lord's, and the fullness thereof."

January 21. You are a great judge of character. Your perfect judgment, which leads you to call forth the best in man, must be trained in demonstration by your constant repetition of this axiom: "Only the good is true and only the true is good."

January 22. You belong among the city's throngs. You teach the nations government. Hold this word: "Shall not the Judge of all the earth do right?"

January 23. What a reasoner for materialism you would make if early in your pathway had not come this text to you: "God is Spirit."

January 24. Seek not the world's applause. To yield to public opinion when you know the true principle of action would cause you to cry: "Would God I had never been born." Keep this for your text: "He leadeth me."

January 25. When you look on a body of people your eyes burn with the controlling fires. Have you learned to train those fires by affirming every morning: "I will guide thee with mine eyes."

January 26. You know how to deal with humanity along mercantile lines. You will keep yourself healthy by declaring that: "No evil can come nigh me. God is my health."

January 27. Home is glad where you love home. "Home without thee cannot be." Keep this word of Jesus: "My yoke is easy."

January 28. You will please the public in whatsoever department of service to it you engage. Keep this text: "I can do all things through Christ which strengtheneth."

January 29. "She is more precious than jewels." "He is known in the gates." Their motto is: "All is well."

January 30. You know your own worth. Others know it too. It is easy for you to master what other men have learned. You should say: "I am strong in Principle."

January 31. You are faithful to duty in whatsoever calling you may be placed - by nature. You will be proficient and efficient by saying always: "I am guided by the Principle of Righteousness."

February

February 1. The world needs your genius. Be faithful in service. Often acknowledge: "I came not to do mine own will, but the will of Him that sent me."

February 2. You can quickly judge right from wrong. Assure yourself and the world of this by mentally holding the word: "My judgments are right."

February 3. Your restless activity signifies the efficiency of your thoughts when you send them forth to accomplish good works. Think much: "Surely as I have thought, so is it come to pass."

February 4. Faithful and true you are. Keep this for your motto: "He is faithful that hath promised."

February 5. Your intuitions are accurate. Walk by them; act upon them. Have your watchword always at hand: "I am purposed that my mouth shall not transgress."

February 6. Keep among the haunts of men. Live where many people may feel the radius of your kindly thoughts. Shine out your soul fire by saying: "Thy kingdom come. Thy will be done."

February 7. Books are readily mastered by you. National resources you can handle wisely. These words held always will put you into the gates of honor: "In Him is Light."

February 8. Beauty is an expression of Divine Goodness. It will increase in you with the years if that Truth be firmly held by you: "He that hath seen me hath seen the Father."

February 9. Loving-hearted are you. Home is your joy. Prove this by the living text: "God is Love."

February 10. Buying and selling merchandise; honorably dealing always, yet always accruing to thine own revenues: "Peace be with thee."

February 11. You are a very useful member of society. Hold on to thy text: "The law of the Lord is perfect; converting the soul."

February 12. It is easy for you to compel people to do your will. Keep hard hold of this truth: "There is only One Will."

February 13. Keep your mind steady to some one purpose or object in life. Thus will your body repose in health: "Thou will keep him in perfect peace whose mind is staid on Thee."

February 14. Whatsoever sphere of service you occupy therein you are earnest and proficient: "I am meek and lowly of heart."

February 15. You could invent things, but instead you patronize inventions. So you are a patron saint. Keep this idea running through all your life: "In Thee I live and move and have my being."

February 16. You are intuitive. You are a good judge of character. You accomplish much good in the world. Let this text abide in you: "I reflect Wisdom, Strength, Holiness from God the Father."

February 17. You are greatly beloved by all who know you while you hold to your axiom: "God is Love."

February 18. Earnest, faithful, kind, you express the kindness of the Divine Parent. Your word is: "The Lord God is my sun and shield."

February 19. Be not anxious about money matters. You will always have abundance if you say daily: "In the Lord's house is much treasure."

February 20. You must have confidence in yourself. Your Self is God. Say this: "All power is given unto me in heaven and in earth."

February 21. You are modest, conscientious, and chaste, by nature. You can be trusted with other people's affairs. Hold this inheritance unspotted by quickening your mind with this confidence: "I am strong in the Lord and the power of His might."

February 22. Be not tenacious of your own will. Be not exacting. Let Go. All is well around you: "Rest in the Lord and He shall bring it to pass.

February 23. Take to a mercantile calling. Get an unusually good education. Hold this word: "I am equal to all occasions."

February 24. You can do a great deal more than you give yourself credit for being able to do. Keep this motto: "I can do all things through Christ." "I am the child of Dominion."

February 25. People and fate are not against you. Cultivate self-respect. You do not need a stronger one to lean on. Say: "God is my strength."

February 26. You need never be dependent upon others for anything of any kind if you will hold this text faithfully: "Jehovah-Jireh - The Lord will provide."

February 27. Let your natural sympathy for the poor and the needy open your purse, for these words held faithfully will keep you always bountifully provided for: 'The Almighty shall be thy defense and thou shalt have plenty of silver."

February 28. Logic is good only when the intuitional judgment accords with it. There is a higher faculty than intellect and sensation. This opens up to you by your repeating much: "God is Spirit. Spirit is Omnipresent."

February 29. Keep your heart and courage up. Divine Goodness folds you round and bears you on. Say often - go to sleep murmuring: "I am charged with Divine Love."

March

March 1. The Spirit of Truth of which Jesus Christ spake continually presseth to whisper into your mind these words: "Be not over careful. Be not anxious. Be not restless. Love Me Best."

March 2.

Kindness, affability, and good sense, these make you worthy. Say daily: "All my help from Thee I bring."

March 3. Because you mean to be right and do right, it seems to you that others must do and be as you say. But regard them as right when they are doing their own business, and keep for your motto: "Mercy, Truth, Love."

March 4. You have a hidden spiritual nature. Keep the intellect still and hush the testimony of the senses, for the enfolding Spirit tells you of immortal things. Let your daily prayer be: "Spirit, teach me."

March 5. Lift up your thoughts to the Presence of God folding you in Goodness. Sing a praise song to Jehovah every day: "I praise Thee. I praise Thee."

March 6. If you do not spend a certain portion of every day speaking unto the Spirit of Goodness you will get materialistic in your tendencies and will lose the charm of living. Speak to the Spirit of God this way: "Thou are here present with me. Blessed be Thy Name."

March 7. Only by having zeal for a righteous cause may you hope to be lifted into high public position and favor. The moment your favor goes to an unrighteous cause you grow from despondency to despondency. Pray this prayer: "My strength is as the strength of ten, because my heart is pure."

March 8. Take special pains to be well educated. Then you will not be inclined to look up to educated people. Take for your motto: "If any man lack wisdom, let him ask of God."

March 9. You have conscientiousness. Let it be known to you that in Righteousness there is no cruelty or domineering; there is large toleration. Here is your prayer: "He giveth to all men liberally, and upbraideth not."

March 10. Listen for that silent nature within you ever whispering of things divine and eternal. Within your own self is your salvation. Keep this truth uppermost: "More than thou canst give to Truth will she on thee confer."

March 11. Love not money. Love God. Honesty is your birthright, pervert not this beautiful principle by believing in the necessity for gain. Keep for your text: "I shall not want."

March 12. Do not be silly about accepting presents from people who love you. Be grateful for assistance offered. Your kindly cheerfulness is ample return. Love is better than money: "I love them that love me."

March 13. Stand alone. Lean on nobody. You know enough to succeed in your own line. Believe in yourself. Say all the time: "I am wise and strong."

March 14. By nature you are upright, honorable, just, sensible affable, kind. These are the principles of Goodness being expressed. Keep your mind clear by holding this thought: "I express God."

March 15. It is easy for you to be a walking encyclopedia. But if you heed the Voice of the Spirit of Truth you will always care more for the Wisdom of Spirit than for the ages of stars. This is your text: "I came forth from God."

March 16. You will always give a just equivalent for all that is rendered unto you. "Let not your heart be troubled." Keep this saying of Jesus Christ: "I came not to do mine own will, but the will of Him that sent me."

March 17. What is for you to do, that you can do. And what you can do, that you must do. Say often: "My help cometh from the Lord."

March 18. Logic is good, but dry. So season yours with knowledge of spiritual laws. This is your text: "My Words are Spirit and Life."

March 19. What made your feet and head pain you was intellectual reasoning. Only a knowledge of Spiritual Truth will heal you. Learn to believe this affirmation of Jesus Christ: "Ye shall know the Truth, and the Truth shall make you free."

March 20. Have unbounded confidence in your own judgment and ability. Be natural. Learn of heavenly things. Say: "The Lord is my keeper."

March 21. You do not need to try to do your work in any other person's way. Do your own way. It is a wise one when your judgment approves. Keep clear of being prejudiced by saying: "My judgment is right."

March 22. Harmony, order, elegance, beauty — these are yours by right. Your word is electrical. You can excel in any department. Do not believe your physician when he tells you that your life forces can be depleted. Declare constantly: "God is my unfailing supply."

March 23. Naturally you are an independent reasoner. Your firmness is not stubbornness. Understand well what you are to do and fear nothing. This should be your controlling thought: "In the way of righteousness is life and in the pathway thereof there is no death."

March 24. Music starts the life forces. Sing some true words while you hear any melody. Sing in the silence of the stringed instrument and the wind instrument. This is your song of songs: "He doeth all things well."

March 25. You do not need to serve in any subordinate capacity. You are capable of managing affairs well your own way. Make this your watchword: "I am Understanding. I am Strength."

March 26. You are educated easily. You reason well. Science and philosophy you are master of. Do not forget that this is your life text: "Mercy and Truth; righteousness and peace, I love."

March 27. Harmony is the dominant key of your quality. Therefore, you may learn music to keep you sound and well. Sing this song silently: "God shall bring every work into judgment."

March 28. People to appeal to you must appeal to your reason. But you must know that some are in the right who cannot give you a reason. Be wide in your mercies. This is your text: "Love endureth all things."

March 29. Your thought is quick. You know speedily. Be patient with those who seem slow-witted. Near you is Jesus Christ. "There's a friend that sticketh closer than a brother." Keep this for your text: "I will guide thee with mine eye."

March 30. You excel in your department. You can keep your head peaceful and free from pain by saying every night as you drop into slumber: "He leadeth me beside still waters."

March 31. Life is ceaseless delight. The Divine Will guides you. Those events that seem disastrous are the pushing aside of some things for others better for your progress in Light. Your prayer should be: "Lead kindly Light."

April

April 1. Pursue faithfully any science and you will become an authority on that branch. But the science of God is the only science that promises complete understanding. Keep this text: "Not the wisdom of this world, nor the prince of this world."

April 2. When your physician threatens you with paralysis, declare vehemently, "God is my unchanging life." But the principal text of your life should be: "The law of Thy mouth is better unto me than thousands of gold and silver."

April 3. Wherever you move you radiate harmony if for your daily text you repeat: "From the rising of the sun unto the going down of the same the Lord's name is to be praised."

April 4. You are noble teacher of science, philosophy, and logic. This is your inheritance. Let nothing wrest your genius from you. Learn this word young: "The works of His hands are verity and judgment; all His commandments are sure."

April 5. The life forces that stir you are the God of you. The activities you demonstrate are Divinely appointed. Let your heart, and will and reason join with this message: "The Lord shall be thine everlasting Light."

April 6. Keep harmonious. By bearing about with you a few texts there will never be any turmoil near you. Keep this one continually: "The Lord shall guide me. In the Lord I delight myself."

April 7. You do not need to serve under another for your own judgment is best. Base all your dealings upon these words: "God is my Wisdom."

April 8. You can reason wisely. If you are full of love, you will master multitudes. Love you must learn to mix with your thoughts. Keep this text: "Peace, peace to him that is far off, and to him that is near, and I will heal him."

April 9. Harmony, music, friends, right amusements, these shall accompany you if you love this text: "I rest in the Lord."

April 10. Spend a certain portion of each day studying something worth while. Keep this text: "Not by might nor by power, but by my Spirit saith the Lord."

April 11. Let no other one's word change your judgment. Act in love. Wear this text down to its spiritual excellence: "I walk with God."

April 12. You are not stubborn. Show that you love those who think you so and they will see you act from judgment. Hold a word for your life law: "The lips of the righteous know what is acceptable."

April 13. When other people's judgment and directions confuse you, listen to your own judgment. It is good. Learn this as Truth: "The law of the Lord is perfect, converting the soul."

April 14. Music and mirth are good. Delight in them as Divine. Carry this motto: "A merry heart doeth good like a medicine." Learn this principle: "The spirit is never crushed. Only the carnal mind droops."

April 15. There is a hidden fire in your nature, which if you turn outward, will guide you into prosperity. Learn how to turn this fire over the world by repeating: "The words that I speak unto you, it is not I that speak, but the Father that dwelleth in me."

April 16. Suppose that nature claims to hurt your brain? Has nature any claim on the Spirit? So you can keep always well and strong by saying: "I lean on Spirit only."

April 17. You are of good council and sound judgment. This judgment is God's way of his own Being shining through you. Say: "I am radiating Wisdom and Love."

April 18. Keep peaceful. Fear nothing and nobody. Rise in the morning and say joyously: "I am strong with the strength of the Spirit."

April 19. You are a natural conqueror. This is God's Being streaming through one gate of your being. Recognize your will as Divine Will and you will make no mistake. Say often: "Not my (human) will but thine be done."

April 20. Let no one lead you. Make all your decisions when you are alone. Be jealous of no one. Rest in the knowledge that there is a principle of Right that rules. Keep this text: "He doeth all things according to Righteousness."

April 21. Your intuitions are good. When you seem to be stubborn it is really an instinctive self -protection you are exercising. Stand for your intuitions. Repeat these words: "God is my Judge."

April 22. When you feel determined to carry out your plans at all hazards, stop to be sure your plan is not the suggestion of somebody else. When it is a righteous scheme you will feel strong and joyous and make others glad also. This is your text: "Counsel is mine and sound wisdom."

April 23. You are so ready with your abilities that you soon become known as a leader among your associates if you learned early this: 'Jesus Christ is all in all."

April 24. Look out for zeal without judgment. Go alone by yourself and decide the question. Keep this text: "God is with me."

April 25. Sympathy is good, but common sense is better. There is an inner witness. Say: "God is my Light."

April 26. Often you catch the thoughts of others among whom you associate. Therefore, take notice of what your judgment spoke early in the morning. Say: "I am wise in Spirit."

April 27. Your life forces generate rapidly. You are a zealous friend, let your morning judgments control your day. Say' at night: "Create in me a clean heart and renew a right spirit within me."

April 28. You have great powers of endurance if you have kept this saying: "I can do all things through Christ." You may be tenacious in your own way when you realize that it is right. Keep this text: "the tongue of the wise is health."

April 29. Your thoughts are copied unaware until you learn this text: "My help cometh from the Lord." You are supremely original when you receive your illumination straight from Principle and not person. Bind this motive to your heart: "God is my sun and my shield."

April 30. Commit to memory your own writings. Study great principles. Trust your silent admonitions. Learn the meaning of this text: "The fear of the Lord is a fountain of life."

May

May 1. Your mind is very strong by nature. Feelings, appetites, and passions must stand aside for that wonderful intuition you were born to. Keep it bright with the words: "God is my Light and my Salvation.

May 2. Your interior judgments concerning business affairs are reliable. Be a foe to no one. Keep this motto: "I trust in God."

May 3. You may start any time to acquire a superior education. Then know that that inner Light of yours is better than books. This is your text: "Take heed to the Spirit."

May 4. Let no other get control over your mind through your affections. There is a fine judgment furnished you by the Spirit of God. Heed it. Say often: "The Lord preserveth them that love Him."

May 5. You are best adapted to the city life. You can learn to be thoroughly independent of other mentalities there. Con over this verse: It may not be my way, It may not be thy way, But sure in His own way The Lord will provide."

May 6. You have fine business intuitions. You seem to be stubborn, but you are not. "Love not pleasure; love God." Keep this axiom: "The secret of the Lord is with them that fear Him."

May 7. You are capable of making superior educational attainments. Decide all important questions on your own solitary judgment. Bear about with you this truth: "Not by might nor by power, but by my Spirit saith the Lord." also this: "I do not believe in the power of evil."

May 8. To conquer is your prerogative. Your mental powers are Godlike. Your business intuitions are accurate. Be sure the special friend you trust is good, for only goodness and greatness will deal fairly with you. Your verse is to be selected by your own judgment from the sixty-second chapter of Isaiah.

May 9. Think over honestly those friendships of yours. Your own way is generally right. Let none other influence you. Keep this life text: "I will walk in Thy Truth."

May 10. Your sympathies are easily enlisted. Your judgment in the early morning must decide your conduct. This is your life motto: "Before they call I (God) will answer and while they are yet speaking I will hear."

May 11. Be never jealous. Be well educated. Listen to your own inner voice. You are a natural leader. Love the principle of Righteousness better than you love people. Keep this text: "Then I consulted with myself."

May 12. Your determination to do whatever you undertake will be your unbounded prosperity if you keep for your life promise these words: "I will guide thee with mine eye."

May 13. Your apparent stubbornness is nature's defense of you. Be sure the cause is just and right which you espouse. This is your inspiration: "I will bless the Lord who hath given me counsel."

May 14. You are zealous and sanguine in your religious views. Be sure you are led by Principle and not by persons. Look out for your judgments. Keep this saying as your own: "I will sing unto the Lord, because he hath dealt bountifully with me."

May 15. Keep a good judgment by trusting your own intuitions. Learn to trust this promise which was selected especially for you: "Thou wilt show me the path of life."... "Thou shalt also be a crown of glory in the hand of the Lord."

May 16. Your life forces swell swiftly. Your recuperative powers are miraculous. Affirm constantly: "I am Spirit, and shed abroad health, life and strength." Believe this text: "In due season we shall reap if we faint not."

May 17. You must be sure of a good education. But your judgment must be based on your own intuitions. Keep this law: "Be not deceived. . . Whatsoever a man soweth that shall he reap."

May 18. Let not feelings, appetites, or passions influence you. Your intuitions are reliable. They are the moving of the Divine Principle through you. Believe in these words: "The Lord shall guide thee continually, and satisfy thy soul in drought."

May 19. If you speak from your inner Light, you will be original in thought and expression; otherwise you will be an imitator. Keep this affirmation: "I speak that I do know and testify that I do understand."

May 20. Be not anxious. Worry about nothing. Be satisfied with the estate whereunto you are called. Learn one basic Truth of Life, and abide by it. Believe in this law: "Seek ye first the kingdom of God and

His righteousness, and all these things shall be added unto you.

May 21. Distrust nobody. Good speakers and lecturers are of your type. Confidence in people will help put you forward. Keep this text: "If the Lord be on our side who can be against us?"

May 22. You belong to the realm of art and mechanics. Get a good education. Fear nobody and nothing. Keep this motto: "Behold, the Lord God will help me; who is he that shall condemn me?"

May 23. What you begin to do, finish it. Understand that continuity and persistence are excellent habits to form. Keep this text: "Blessed are they that keep my ways."

May 24. There is nothing around you to make you dissatisfied. It is all your own state of mind, wholly subject to your will. Learn books. Learn Principles. Rest in the Law of Goodness as impartial. Keep this word: "The Lord reigneth."

May 25. You must learn some one thing well. Compel yourself to be faithful to that one duty. Principles are eternal. This is your affirmation: "I abide in Truth."

May 26. You must have a superior education. Compel yourself to be faithful to whatever you promise to perform. Learn this Principle: "The Good reigns."

May 27. You are fitted to speak in public when principles enthuse you. Carry nothing to extremes except your understanding of Divine Law. Bear this in mind: "There shall be no evil happen to the just."

May 28. Your cheerfulness and vivacity will abide with you if you are absorbed in this Law: "Understanding is a wellspring of life unto him that hath it."

May 29. Learn to be satisfied with the way the law works. Mind what is true. That which you begin, finish it. Make your life text: "The Lord God hath opened mine ear, and I was not rebellious."

May 30. You may finish your text books word for word. Meanwhile be aware that there is a Principle instructing you, and which you can use any time, that makes you master of books beyond what they teach. Believe this law: "The righteous shall be recompensed in the earth."

May 31. Be constant in friendship, faithful in marriage, and diligent in business. Resist your temptation to inconstancy. Bear these words in mind: "I am the Lord, I change not."

June

June 1. Your very arms and hands express your thoughts. So you are known and read of all. Therefore take this text: "Let the thoughts of my heart be right."

June 2. You are a maker of your associates. Form a good opinion of their worthy traits and hold steadily to them, eschewing the evil. This is your text: "There shall no evil happen to the just."

June 3. Your activities express the quick power you possess. Learn a good science and also invent a machine. This is your life text: "The hope of the righteous shall be gladness."

June 4. You are mechanical in genius. Make something entirely new. Let your mind learn the law of peace. Get a good education. Keep this affirmation: "The righteous shall flourish like a branch."

June 5. You may know all things by a little persistence. Therefore, cultivate persistence. Get a good idea of what you can do and carry it out. Keep this word: "I am satisfied with myself."

June 6. You have knowledge. This is well. Learn mechanics. You can invent something. Be not restless. Manage your affairs with steadiness. Keep this motto: "The thoughts of the diligent tend only to plenteousness."

June 7. Your thoughts affect powerfully the people around you. Therefore, be sure your thoughts are strictly true. Keep steady, constant, cool headed. Learn this law: "Wisdom is the principal thing; therefore get Wisdom; and with all thy getting get understanding.

June 8. Be very persistent in finishing the studies you attempt. Resist your temptation to changeableness. You affect people near you strongly; therefore learn Truth. By steadiness of purpose, you preside over nations. Keep this text: "All power is given unto me in heaven and in earth."

June 9. Your mind makes speakers and lecturers. Therefore, be wise in judgment by often repeating: "The Lord God hath given me the tongue of the learned, that I should know how to speak a word in season."

June 10. Never distrust anybody. Find out men's good qualities and keep your mind on them, not on their failings. This will give you a great light. Learn this affirmation: "I am governed by the Principle of Goodness and fear no evil happenings."

June 11. Restlessness is the outpicturing of quick powers of some kind. Make up your mind what you want to do and persist in accomplishing it. Keep this saying: "He shall deliver thee in six troubles, yea in seven there shall no evil touch thee."

June 12. You have mechanical genius hiding within your nature. Faithful adherence to every duty will quicken it into flame. Learn this inspiring principle: "The

Salvation of the righteous is of the Lord; He is their strength in time of trouble."

June 13. Keep steady courage. Be cheerful in principle. There is no credit to you for smiling when there is plenty to smile at - no; smile in spite of fate. So you will be great and beloved. This is your life text: "The Lord God will help me; therefore have I set my face like a flint."

June 14. You may do faithfully each day what belongs to you whether you like it or not, for it is the only way you can earn the fruit of your life. Be cheerful by determining to be cheerful. This is labor that conquers. Keep this motto: "Blessed is he that waiteth."

June 15. Be strong, and of good courage. Your lot is not unfortunate, but on the contrary, is your best training ground; so be brave and fearless. This is your text to live by: "Yea the Almighty shall be thy defense, and thou shalt have plenty of silver."

June 16. Every movement of yours tells of energy needing to be expressed by perfect thoughts. Therefore, learn what is absolutely true. Then your thoughts will fall all about the people near you like rains of refreshment. Keep this truth night and day: "My kindness shall not depart from thee."

June 17. Never be suspicious of anybody. The more you believe in them the surer they will be to do right by you. This ought to be your motto: "Shall not the judge of all the earth do right?"

June 18. Be simple; be natural. Trust in the law of the Right. You are always to be sustained by this message: "I am with you always."

June 19. Your nature can be trained to be satisfied and at peace. Therefore, while doing the best you can be not restless; be at peace. Keep this word close: "There shall no evil happen to the just."

June 20. Learn what you like to do best and stand by that till you perfect yourself in it. Be not inconstant. Pray much. Keep this word: "My fruit is better than gold, yea than fine gold."

June 21. You are kind and loving. You do not like to be dictated to and you need not so be, for your judgment is good. This is your text: "Pleasant words are health to the bones."

June 22. If you are rightly trained in your thoughts, you have become strong and self-reliant. By keeping this text you are getting on in power: "Thou God seest me."

June 23. It is sensitiveness that causes you to seem queer and eccentric sometimes. So this verse ought to be constantly in your heart: "I am sufficient unto myself, being "strong in the Lord."

June 24. You can learn to help those people you do not like by bearing this text in mind: "I do not believe in weakness; I believe in Strength and Goodness."

June 25. You are a healing presence to all because you love your home and friends. Keep this text close in your heart: "Surely goodness and mercy shall follow me all the days of my life."

June 26. Hoard up nothing. You will never come to want. Love of Divine Omnipresence will make you to draw from the ends of the universe things for your use. This is your heritage from the Principle of Love: "The earth is full of the goodness of the Lord."

June 27. Be not anxious about money matters. As you provide for your children or for those you love so Divine Love provides for you. Keep this text: "The Lord is my shepherd, I shall not want."

June 28. All who come near you love you, therefore you should draw all your love to return unto them from the Divine Presence. Keep this text: 'How excellent is thy loving kindness, O God! therefore, the children of men put their trust under the shadow of thy wings.

June 29. Persist in the studies you began. Learn that you are loveable and so your quaintnesses are loveable. If you understand Divine Love, you are a healing radiance among the people: "Delight thyself also in the Lord; and he shall give thee the desires of thine heart."

June 30. Be full of courage in all you undertake, for if you trust in the law of Goodness you will have great success. Keep this word: "Trust in the Lord, and do good; so shalt thou dwell in the land, and verily thou shalt be fed."

July

July 1. With your loving all people because God is Love, you will heal, and feed and comfort by your presence. Get your reinforcements from Spirit. Lean on this law: "The Lord shall help them."

July 2. Your plans will always succeed if you have this text always in your faith: "The Lord shall help me and deliver me."

July 3. Your home is your haven of rest and there they must love you fondly for you love them. Be never anxious, for "The Lord will provide" for you always, because you are diligent. Keep this text: "No weapon that is formed against thee shall prosper."

July 4. Your faithfulness to duty will bring you success even if it is when it will seem to you late. This is a life word written for you: "I will make an everlasting covenant with you, even the sure mercies of David."

July 5. You are by nature warm and loving, therefore you heal by kindly thoughts. Keep this text: "The tongue of the wise is health."

July 6. When you know the absolute Truth you will never be worn or disheartened by people near you. Here is your strong law: "I am strong with the Strength of the Spirit. I am alive with the Life of the Spirit."

July 7. Let nobody wear upon or fret you. Back of you is the Infinite Source of Life, Health, and Strength. Pass along the bountiful supplies of Divine Goodness to your neighbor. This is your motto: "God works through me to will and to do all that ought to be done by me."

July 8. There is no reason for you to care and fear lest you should not be provided for. The less you take anxious thought the more success you will have. Hear this thought in the soul: "Cast all your care on God."

July 9. There is much love in your heart, therefore you are a healing to children. The trust of a little child in its parents should be the nature of your trust in Divine Love. Keep this text: "I will never leave thee, nor forsake thee."

July 10. Your perseverance is noble. You can make it agreeable by bearing this word in your heart: "There is no reality in evil."

July 11. There is a lovely talent hiding within your nature. Let it shine forth by shedding abroad this word continually: "God is my Light and my inspiration."

July 12. There is a Christ way of healing the sick, which you can learn very readily because your heart is kind and tender. These words spoken by you will accomplish much: "I love all the world."

July 13. There is a quality about you, which will make you successful without anxiety. Therefore, "trust in the Lord and . . . verily thou shalt be fed." Keep this word: "In righteousness shalt thou be established."

July 14. Remember that all people are Sons and daughters of God. None of them need to disturb your peace of mind. You have peace, health, and love enough to give them all. Learn this law: "In my Father's house is enough and to spare."

July 15. Make a home for yourself and keep it by holding determinedly to this truth: "Omnipotent Love cannot be changed or interfered with."

July 16. Your making up your mind to do the right thing will make you strong to carry out your determinations successfully always. Keep this text: "As thy day is so shall thy strength be."

July 17. No matter how people seem to look upon you, you may be sure that they will think nobly of you always if you bear this law in your heart: "I am governed by the law of God."

July 18. You are strong, and firm, and fine by nature. Let this strength and noble firmness clothe you by your saying: "Jesus Christ is all in all."

July 19. There is no power in evil of any kind to overcome you. There is no substance in material conditions to hurt you. Keep this axiom: "My God is the rock of my refuge."

July 20. Be afraid of nothing that you eat, drink, or wear. Step boldly out into whatever line of business you choose. Wear this shield in your heart: "We shall not die - we are Spirit and not flesh forever more."

July 21. Think in orderly fashion the exact truth. This habit will make you a wonderful healer when you do not hardly realize it. You can understand this by believing that: "I am the healing Life."

July 22. By nature, your thoughts are independent. Nobody can misunderstand your motives, or distrust your goodness if you keep this text: "God is my portion."

July 23. Keep as the gift of Supreme Goodness that fine intuitive judgment. Act by it. Trust it. Let this be your daily affirmation: "There is a light that lighteth every man that cometh into the world."

July 24. When you love, people trust in their Goodness. Trust by reason of this principle - we make people honest by believing in their honesty. Then bear about all the time this truth: "There shall no ill come nigh thy dwelling."

July 25. People may say of you that you lack natural policy. This is a good accusation. It means that you are defended by the Divine Goodness. Wear this text: "Resist not evil."

July 26. There is one positive rule of life, which you may observe till you are supremely successful. It is this: "Thy Father which seeth in secret shall reward thee openly."

July 27. You observe everything you see and it changes your thoughts. Stop this, and do and think according to Principle. Here is your law: "Every one of us shall give account of himself to God."

July 28. Control your feelings and your judgment will always stand out clear and accurate. Mind this word: "My salvation shall not tarry."

July 29. How orderly and harmonious is your nature! Therefore, you will prosper on the Principle: "The words that I speak unto you, it is not I that speak but the Father that dwelleth in me."

July 30. You love to associate with many people sharing like the Apostles "all things in common." So you ought to think this truth all the time: "There is no respect of persons with God."

July 31. Learn self-control and you will show forth extraordinary powers. Abide by this principle: "Fearing nothing I push onward to 'the mark of the high calling'."

August

August 1. Sit by yourself often and mentally deny that any evil can have power over you or any material conditions hinder you. Above all, use the fifth universal denial. Then you will never be deceived by anybody. This is it: "There is no sin, sickness, or death in Spirit and in Truth."

August 2. The world you think of is your ideal. The world about you will never hurt or hinder you if you keep this Truth in mind: "I am governed by the Principle of Righteousness and am not afraid."

August 3. Let no sadness get possession of you ever. Such a state of mind would be what somebody's near presence had effected and not truly yours. So you ought to make this your daily word: "Praise the Lord for His goodness unto me."

August 4. By nature, you are refined like gold and none can truly spoil you. Be strong in the Principle of Righteousness. Trust the Divine Goodness every minute. Keep this word: "No weapon that is formed against thee shall prosper."

August 5. Learn a great principle and trust it constantly, then your thoughts will never be changed by the thoughts of those with whom you associate. This is the principle that will keep you: "I am folded round with Divine Truth."

August 6. Order and harmony you delight in. This is your nature. All your affairs will be prosperous and harmonious if you hold this motto: "In me is the kingdom of heaven."

August 7. Who is that one who wins your heart? Trust in that one as guided by the love of righteousness until there is absolute safety in all the friendship - all the confidence. This is your life text: "God, thy God, has anointed thee with the oil of gladness."

August 8. You are strong in Spirit. You are bold in Truth. You are great in

Goodness. Demonstrate all this by believing this: "Jesus Christ is my friend."

August 9. The people around you will be strong and well if you will be true to Truth. This is your special truth: "God is my unfailing Health and my unchanging Life."

August 10. As an author, as a teacher, as a student you can be a success. As a merchant, you will not fail. Therefore, shine forth with your golden gifts. These words are your talisman: "There is no power in evil to hurt me. There is no substance in matter to hinder me."

August 11. Sometimes you speak from the thoughts and suggestions of your friends unless you are well grounded into this principle: "The Lord thy God in the midst of thee is mighty."

August 12. Let not your tongue slip into words against your neighbors. When one could be made true by a true word of yours, speak it though it may seem to sever you from some tie. This is your life text: "I will speak Truth forever."

August 13. Life in sweet peace is your privilege. This you may secure by keeping this word: "The Lord is in the midst of thee; thou shalt not see evil any more."

August 14. There is strength and energy in your constitution. The repetition of these words will cause you to demonstrate strength and energy: "God is not the God of the dead, but of the living."

August 15. There is Divine Love in your heart. This love can be made to show forth as the health and joyous life of your neighbors by your believing in this Truth: "The Father that dwelleth in me He doeth the works."

August 16. Though all the people conspire to put you down, yet you still are filled with noble aspiration: "Underneath are the everlasting arms."

August 17. You are persistent and determined by nature. Get a mighty truth to demonstrate and base your actions on a noble resolve. This is your inherited text: "Thy faith hath saved thee."

August 18. There is great inherent power in your mind. Use it wisely by learning to square all your life's actions by this rule: "Render therefore unto Caesar the things which are Caesar's, and unto God the things that are God's."

August 19. You have boldness and faith. When you have made this text your axiom you will demonstrate success: "The Lord thinketh upon me. He is my help and my deliverer. The Lord be magnified."

August 20. There are no environments or events that can hold you down. You rise by inherent excellence. This is your birthright: "In God have I put my trust; I will not be afraid what man can do unto me."

August 21. Your friendships must not be allowed to warp your judgment. Keep wise in righteousness by this law: "God shall send forth His mercy and His truth."

August 22. Your intuitions are correct. You do not need to suffer from the hard facts of life, for your mind is Creator of your environments. This message is for you: "The lines are fallen unto me in pleasant places; yea, I have a goodly heritage."

August 23. Your mind is keen and discriminating. Your ideas are accurate. Your affections are pure. Learn this life rule: "The Lord rewardeth me according to my righteousness... Therefore has the Lord girded me with strength."

August 24. Harmonious combinations delight you. Harmony may surround you all the days of your life if you will believe this: "The Lord my God will enlighten my darkness."

August 25. No low conditions of human experience could spoil your nobility of character and mind, once you have learned this rule: "There is no power in evil to hurt me and no action of sin can defile me while I know them as a lie from the beginning."

August 26. You impart harmony and rest. You are lovely in character. This you demonstrate daily by repeating these words: "Goodness and mercy shall follow me all the days of my life."

August 27. Be sure you are in the right and that is quite enough. Try to control no one but yourself. Rest in this law: "The Lord will give strength unto his people."

August 28. You do not ever need to experience pain or receive a hurt of any kind. Nature has provided you beautifully with defensives. Use them by holding these words in mind: "I had fainted unless I had believed to see the goodness of the Lord in the land of the living."

August 29. You are a radiator of health and harmony and peace if you love this law: "God is the strength of my heart."

August 30. Your strong likes and dislikes are your protection. Nevertheless, you ought to say this: "With God is no respect of persons."

August 31. What mighty endurance you have! Shed it abroad over the earth for the people to refresh themselves with strength by putting forth daily these words: "Thou hast declared thy strength among the people."

September

September 1. You have great self-control and do not need to attempt to control others for your example is enough. Bear this truth in mind: "The Lord shall give that which is good; and our land shall yield her increase."

September 2. When you love, you worship. Your will is strong. Your powers are remarkable. Your verse is to be found in Isaiah 54. **September 3.** Were it not for your intuition and reasoning, you would be materialistic. Learn this principle to live by: "God works with me and through me and by me and for me."

September 4. If you will learn to love the Principle of Righteousness better than anything or anybody in all the world you will succeed in all things. This is your text: "No weapon that is formed against thee shall prosper."

September 5. You can make wonderful attainments along your line if you hold this text: "In righteousness there is prosperity."

September 6. Your judgments are quick and right. By this you show that this text is your own: "Thy righteousness shall go before thee; the glory of the Lord shall be thy reward."

September 7. Your intuitions are good. Your affections are kind and true. But unless you love Principle better than personality you will have sorrow of heart. This text will help you to be strong: "Then shalt thou call and the Lord shall answer."

September 8. When you seem to be cast down then you are about to spring highest. Bear this axiom in mind: "The Lord shall guide thee continually."

September 9. Harmony and peace are round about you. You shed them abroad. Keep cheerful and trusting. Love this text best: "I and the Father are one."

September 10. The love of righteousness will protect and defend you from yourself. Keep this text: "Delight thyself in the Lord and He will cause thee to ride upon the high places of the earth."

September 11. Your interior nature is fine and sensitive. Your thoughts are idealistic. Keep this text and you will be happy: "Greatly beloved, understand the words that I speak unto thee."

September 12. You are like refined gold. All the people will realize this if you understand this message that follows you always: "Peace be unto thee, be strong, yea be strong."

September 13. You have great self-control. You control others also. But you had better teach them strong principles and let them control themselves. This is your motto: "If God be for us who can be against us?"

September 14. You understand nature well. You are quick and accurate in all things except your friendships. You are able to be wise in these also by holding this affirmation: "I am governed by the law of the Good and cannot fear sin or evil."

September 15. Music and harmony enchant you. Discord troubles you. Discord and inharmony need never come into your lot if you abide in this Truth: "I am in the midst of Israel — my people shall never be ashamed."

September 16. Merge your great will into the Divine Will. Then your character will be beautiful beyond description. Repeat this pledge: "Not my will, but thine, be done."

September 17. Like silver tried — like gold refined, so is your fortitude. This will make life delightful for you: "The motive is its own justification; my motive is pure. Therefore I am justified."

September 18. When you determine to control yourself, understand that it is God's control and you will rise in joy and wisdom. This is your life fiat: "Let Divine Wisdom now be demonstrated by the perfect judgment with which I administer upon affairs."

September 19. It is not so necessary as you imagine that you have somebody to love. No. Love the law of the Eternal Principle working through you and you will be utterly satisfied. Repeat this affirmation: "I am the Idea of God, and in God I live and move and have my being."

September 20. Though your environments design to crush you, yet shall you see yourself rising with greatness greater than them all. You rise by this affirmation: "I am governed by the law of God and cannot swerve from the path wherein He hath placed me."

September 21. Instead of analyzing nature, investigate the Spirit of God. Bear this in mind: "Not by might nor by power, but by my Spirit saith the Lord."

September 22. How quickly the meaning and purpose of a book lie open to your knowledge. Let all this quick perceptiveness be employed in the investigation of the Divine Order. This affirmation will be life to you, and strength for those with whom you associate: "In the Lord Jehovah is everlasting strength."

September 23. So long as you follow your intuitions, you cannot be deceived. When you follow the vanity of pleasure seeking your judgment is lost. Above all notice what is right for you to do by others. "Whoso stoppeth his ears at the cry of the poor, (the desolate hearted) he also shall cry himself, but shall not be heard." Your verse is in Malachi 2.

September 24. If you are strictly moral you will never come to want. There is a close connection in your life between the Principle of Goodness and success. This is your text: "The lip of truth shall be established forever."

September 25. Love not excitement. Love great principles. Take strict care of your obligations to others. Bear your affirmation constantly in mind: "The righteous shall never be removed. The hope of the righteous shall be gladness."

September 26. You must learn not to be influenced by the mental conditions of other people. You must know what is right and abide by it. Keep this promise in mind: "There shall no evil happen to the just."

September 27. You are by nature just and honest in all your dealings. You are fine in your intuitions. Be not afraid to trust your own judgment unbiased by anybody. This must be your life text: 'Righteousness keepeth him that is upright in his way."

September 28. Overcome your skeptical and materialistic tendencies by constantly remembering that there must be a Creative Principle and that It must be Intelligence and Goodness. This is your affirmation: "Wait on the Lord; be of good courage, and He shall strengthen thine heart."

September 29. Within your mind is a world of equity and harmony. This thought world it is your privilege to externalize.

Remember this text: "Thou shalt decree a thing and it shall be established unto thee."

September 30. Permit no melancholy to settle down over your mind. Your own ideals can be carried out by you. Trust them. Lean hard on the Divine Presence. Speak these words often: "In righteousness shalt thou be established."

October

October 1. Fine abilities came into being with your being. Your true judgments are unbiased ones. Use your own intuitions. Let nothing tempt you to be either unjust or sensual: "I am upright in heart."

October 2. When you are studying everything so carefully think of it all as but the sign and symbol of great spiritual realities. Then look over into the realities by saying daily: "My word shall prosper in the thing whereto I sent it."

October 3. You do not need to give a reason for anything. That which you know because you do know it is right. Silence is your greatest weapon of defense. Believe this text: "The Lord shall guide thee continually and satisfy thy soul in drought."

October 4. The outer world is subject to your slightest wish if you believe this affirmation: "I can preach the gospel. I can heal the sick. I can cast out demons. I can raise the dead."

October 5. It is easy for you to imitate others. Now if you will make some supreme statements of Truth you will see ideals finer than what your neighbors dictate, and will be a greater help to the world. Here is your text: "I cast all my care on God. He careth for me."

October 6. You can readily master all languages. There is one language you must be sure to learn — viz: the language of Spirit. This is your life principle: "I would speak to the Almighty, and I reason with God."

October 7. You must hold firm rein over your temper. Stop often in the midst of your tasks to say: "I do believe that Divine Goodness leads me and loves me."

October 8. A high temper is an energy waiting for a good motive to hurl it into the world to work out some mighty purpose. You must hurl yours forth on the wings of these words: "I know that I shall be justified."

October 9. Activity need never waste your powers if you hold to this as absolutely true: "My words are life to them that find them, and health to all their flesh."

October 10. Sit down quietly every day and in the silence wait patiently for some true word to fall into your mind. This word will guide you aright. There will be no failure or misfortune in your lot. Say this always and under all circumstances: "I praise the Lord."

October 11. If you choose to do right and choose true friends, you will always have plenty of drops of gold. Your mental state is responsible for all your environments and all your possessions. Keep this law in your heart: "Thy words were found and I did eat them, and thy word was unto me the joy and rejoicing of my heart: for I am called by thy name, O Lord God of hosts."

October 12. Let not melancholy ever seize you, for your finest ideals you are supremely capable of carrying out. This word carried in your heart will take you safely through everything: "I am with thee to save thee and to deliver thee saith the Lord."

October 13. You are inventive. You can make original designs. If you become very spiritually minded your externalization of your ideals will be wonderful. These words are sent for your daily food: "Thou shalt be in league with the stones of the field; and the beasts of the field shall be at peace with thee."

October 14. You can write your deep thoughts and by and by they will show how quickening your soul fires are. Keep this word: " The Lord God hath given me the tongue of the learned."

October 15. The higher mathematics are very simple to you. Therefore, study them. Get familiar with the highest truths of the profoundest mystics. Believe this: "All power is given unto me."

October 16. Learn the moral law. This will make you successful. You need not anticipate trouble. The Spirit of Goodness will keep you from affliction if you trust It.

Here is a divine leading for you: "Let us not be weary in well doing."

October 17. When the temptation to skepticism seizes you take these sayings: "Not the wisdom of this world. The wisdom of this world is foolishness with God. . . . The spiritual man judgeth all things."

October 18. When you have thought profoundly upon any subject, do not hesitate to speak in public all that is in your mind to tell the people. This is your mission. One affirmation will set you into great power. It is this: "The Lord God hath given me the tongue of the learned, that I should know how to speak a word in season."

October 19. Your true nature is just and honorable. All people can trust you. Bear these words in your mind daily: "With thee is the fountain of life; in thy light shall we see light."

October 20. You can master the languages. You can invent machines. You do not need to be influenced by the minds of those near you, for there is a power of the

Spirit always with you. Say this often: "There is a Spirit in man and the inspiration of the Almighty giveth him understanding."

October 21. How noble is your quick judgment when unbiased by associations. This is your law of life: "Blessed are they that keep my ways."

October 22. Never let any personality control your judgment or your consciousness. Rise on the wings of your own spiritual convictions. Keep this text in mind: "I will not fear though there be an host encamped against me."

October 23. Never be jealous. Never be pretentious or proud. Be meek and lowly of heart. Bear this your natal verse in mind every minute: "Hear, for I will speak of excellent things, and the opening of my lips shall be right things."

October 24. When you are looking up to one whom you consider learned in books, remember that to be wise in Spirit is greater than all other wisdom. Here is your affirmation: "There is One Spirit - One Only. I am Spirit."

October 25. You are capable of managing large affairs. Those whom you serve can trust you. You will always be sure of competence in all things if you repeat this text daily: "The Almighty shall be thy defense, and thou shalt have plenty of silver."

October 26

Some will call you cold and exacting. This nature is only what seems. Deep within your soul is the God light of reason. Heed it. So you will be good and do good. This is your verse: "God is Love - God is Spirit - God is Truth - God is Life."

October 27. Never be tyrannical. To be so hides the beams of the sun of Righteousness and you cannot realize Life at its best. Keep this word: "I am thy God and will still give thee aid."

October 28. You do not need to look up to anybody. You do not need to govern anybody. You can have but one Lord, and that is Jesus Christ. You can govern only one and that is yourself. This is your text: "Love is the fulfilling of the law."

October 29. If you will regard the healing power you possess as being of Divine origin and office, you will never lose it. Keep your thoughts on Spiritual themes. Love this text: "Thou shalt hear a voice behind thee, saying: This is the way, walk ye in it."

October 30. You are an effective public speaker by inherent power. Lean hard on the Almighty and demonstrate the baptism of the Holy Spirit and say: "Whom have I in heaven but thee, and there is none on earth whom I desire beside thee."

October 31. "Be thou faithful unto death." This text will keep you true to your home: "Love not pleasure, love God." Remember continually this truth: "There is in man a higher love than love of happiness; he can do without happiness, and instead thereof find blessedness."

November

November 1. You are a skillful operator. Keep in mind that all your outward actions define a noble spiritual work and signal an operation of Soul. Keep this law: "Thy words only I give forth, for I hear Thy command, 'Acquaint now thyself with me'."

November 2. Never try to enforce your government by tyranny. God is no tyrant. You are commanded to be Godlike. This is your verse: "He shall lift up his voice for the oppressed."

November 3. Never give way to anger or grief or jealousy. Take such feelings at their worst and speak some Divine truth instead of the angry, or grieved or jealous word. This is a saving Truth: "God is now working with me and through me and by me and for me."

November 4. Be just. Be considerate. Be merciful. You had better give up the punishments you meditate than carry them out. Keep this text for your own: "Why have ye made the heart... sad, whom I have not made sad, saith the Lord."

November 5. If you praise the Divine Spirit, you will be much praised. If you praise the Divine Spirit, you will learn to be merciful. Learn the deep intention of your verse: "I will have mercy, and not sacrifice."

November 6. Learn self-government. This is your first step toward power, wisdom, and strength. Look upon the changes that are taking place in nations, societies, and individuals, as the divine order of things. Bear this word daily: "Hear thou from the heavens their prayer and maintain their cause."

November 7. If you learn the law of God, you will trust that all people will do it when you announce it without your enforcing it. This text held constantly will train you to mercy: "The Lord render to every man his righteousness and his faithfulness."

November 8. "Deny thyself" exactly as Jesus Christ meant. Learn what He meant. Your silence will be the majesty of your name. While so silent, think persistently this thought: "I shall put my Spirit in you, and ye shall live."

November 9. You can fill government offices. Before your God, you must walk blameless if you would see your deepest wish granted. You will secure all things by prayer. Keep this prayer constantly: "Thy kingdom come; Thy will be done."

November 10. No one will ever be treacherous to you. No one will ever fail you, if you learn this precept young: "With all thy getting, get understanding."

November 11. You will get praise and honor among the people where you dwell by believing this message: "It shall come to pass that while they are yet speaking I will hear. Praise ye the Lord."

November 12. Love the knowledge of Spirit best. The rest of the Soul in God is the best rest. Labor conquers all things. Speak the merciful, just, tender word when you are tempted to speak otherwise. This is your natal note: "The greatness of the kingdom under the whole heaven shall be given to the people of the saints of the Most High."

November 13. How strong your nature is! Consecrate it today to the Spirit of God. This Spirit will guide you into prosperity and joy. Repeat this text until it is bone of your bone: "My help cometh from the Lord, which made heaven and earth."

November 14. Your vitality will increase and your heart shall rest in peace if you keep this in faith: "He that keepeth thee will not slumber."

November 15. Be sure to stop and consider well before you make any move, which will hurt or grieve another. There is a Principle of Goodness waiting for you to be one with it in action, speech, and thought. Here is your word: "Whom have I in heaven but thee? I love and adore Thee above all things."

November 16. No arbitrary plan carried out by you will make you happy. The love of God reigning in you will make you supremely glad. Keep this text: "I have given thee for a witness to the people."

November 17. Be careful to be merciful. Mercy and Truth are loving, and healing. Repeat this daily: "Divine Love is good to all."

November 18. Justice administered by you will be justice indeed if you keep this for your life text: "The power of the Holy Spirit is on me."

November 19. Merge your strong will into the Divine Will by saying daily: "Divine Will. Divine Will. I trust to the Divine Will that endureth forever."

November 20. No jealousy, no temper, no strong emotion will spoil or hinder you if you bear about always your Scripture verses: "Thy sins be forgiven thee - My peace I leave with thee."

November 21. Anger has no hold on you. Sadness never conquers you. Hatred will not rest in your bosom ever if your remember this: "My soul doth magnify the Lord."

November 22. Spare no pains or money to be well educated in what the world estimates highly. But above all, know this: "Wisdom is the knowledge of God. Love is the fulfilling of the law."

November 23. When you are found to be in the wrong, acknowledge it meekly. This will keep you from being wrong next time. Be strictly truthful. Stop to see if what you tell is true. All your powers and especially your vision, depend upon your truthfulness. Say this often: "I am just and true."

November 24. In the early morning, you may have true visions of things pending if you are steadfast to this word: "He is our peace, who hath made one, and hath broken down the middle wall of partition."

November 25. Never be an enemy to anybody for as such you would be unjust. Be trustful of even those who seem to be at enmity with you. Be loving to all. Make it your principle of life. Also keep this affirmation: "God is the speech of my tongue, the thought of my heart, and the strength of my right hand."

November 26. Be sure that the cause you espouse is a righteous one for you are very faithful to whatever you espouse. This is your rightful principle of faith: "All they that know thy name will put their trust in thee; for thou, Lord, hast not forsaken them that seek thee."

November 27. You can easily make any great undertaking worthwhile. Do not wait for a leader to direct you. Ask the Divine Guidance and push ahead with your convictions. Bear this text about with you as a living Principle: "Seek ye the kingdom of God; and all these things shall be added unto you."

November 28. Speak from impulse if you have well trained your mind by these words: "I am with thee saith the Lord." "I will betroth thee unto me in righteousness."

November 29. People with one idea at a time, like you, can regulate a whole community by silently praying this prayer three times per day: "I thank thee that thou hast heard me." ... "Many shall be purified, and made white, and tried."

November 30. Train yourself not to act from impulse. Conserve the energy of your feelings into these words intensely spoken: "I am strong in righteousness."

December

December 1. Let your extraordinary prophetic instincts be trained to foresee only the good, and let your acquaintance with Divine Spirit make you a power against evil. Say often: "Nothing can hinder the Spirit of Goodness from reigning supreme."

December 2. You may be as zealous and optimistic in your undertakings as you please if you repeat this truth daily: "No weapon that is formed against me shall prosper... righteousness is of me, saith the Lord."

December 3. There is great harmony in your being. You are a faithful friend. The way you go is ordained for your training. You can have gold and friendships as tokens of Divine favor if you believe in this promise: "Thou shalt be far from oppression: for thou shall not fear."

December 4. You are sympathetic, loving, devoted, and kind. This is the Spirit of God flowing down through you. All your words will be right words if you hold this as true: "With great mercies will I gather thee."

December 5. You must not mind opposition at all. Your mind will hold its own and be always light and free if you say: "I do not believe in the power of evil."

December 6. Notice what people mean when they speak to you. Then let your conclusions be accurate, not careless. There are certain studies you ought to pursue. The study of spiritual laws will lead you into the right understanding of all things. This is your special truth: "I have given thee for a witness to the people, a leader and commander to the people."

December 7. Give many days to music. So will the harmony of your soul thoughts be wakened. No other way for you to express perfectly your Divinity. These words will quicken your harmonies in some wonderful way: "I am the perfect child of the living God, spiritual, harmonious, free, fearless."

December 8. Strength and honor and good judgment and leadership you will realize if you repeat every day boldly: "My strength is in me. I am the Lord; I change not. I know what is right and there is no fault in me."

December 9. Your mind is active to gather conclusions quickly. You may be supremely accurate by learning the Divine law of the Spirit among us. The spiritual doctrine at its highest you should learn. It is this: "He that hath seen me hath seen the Father." "I and the Father are One."

December 10. The secret of the Lord it is for you to know. There is that about you that will lead you into it. "Then your joy no man taketh from you." Keep this for your daily text: "Incline your ear, and come unto me: hear and your soul shall live."

December 11. Let people fully state their propositions before you answer them. Then you will be wiser in your answers. Keep saying always: "Ye shall know in that day that I am He that doth speak; Behold, it is I."

December 12. Speak not forth from your own interpretations of people's sayings, until you have been trained by this principle: "The Lord shall guide thee continually, and satisfy thy soul in drought."

December 13. Early in the morning, you may foresee events if you have learned the highest law of Truth. "Prophecy is yours and sound judgment." This truth will help you: "God judgeth in the earth."

December 14. You can carry out any plan you please. You have executive genius. Your plans will be original and masterful if you train your spiritual forces by these words: "Cast thy burden upon the Lord, and he shall sustain thee."

December 15

You do not mind opposition, no matter who opposes you, if you make this text your rule of life: "I do not believe in failure; I believe only in prosperity."

December 16. Because you can hold one idea at a time steadfastly it is necessary that you hold an absolute Truth firmly if you would be supremely successful. Hold this for your prosperous thought: "I rejoice in my strong Spirit of Love."

December 17

You will believe in plenty of gold and silver and laugh at poverty if you do hold daily: "The Almighty is my defense and I have plenty of all things."

December 18

Drop out of mind your belief in the future for good things and events to come to you. Affirm that they are already in your grasp. You will learn the principle of "nowness" by repeating these words of Jesus Christ: "Believe that ye receive."

December 19. Go carefully in repeating what is told you. Better not to tell anything that is told you. You will conserve great energy in truth by repeating this word: "Truth is my shield and buckler."

December 20. Yield gently and graciously when you are found to be in the wrong. Then you will never be in the wrong. Keep saying these words till all the things you like are gathered to you as steel filings are gathered to a magnet: "I am full of joy in the Love of God."

December 21. Naturally, you are at the head of business affairs. Your judgment will always serve you perfectly if you have trained yourself into goodness by this thought: "Giving thanks always for all things unto God and the Father in the name of our Lord Jesus Christ."

December 22

Your deep spiritual nature abides in thoughts of the real and eternal. There shall no ill come nigh such as you if you remember who provides for your every need. Keep this thought reigning: "Thou art my All."

December 23. You can indeed carry into the realm of the external your beautiful ideals. All that is necessary is persistence in this idea: "My word shall prosper in the thing whereunto I send it."

December 24. Your greatness will be demonstrated before all the people if you bear this idea as your ruling one: "He that is greatest among you shall be your servant."

December 25. You are full of the love of doing good. Your doings always show good judgment if you often say these words: "Let Divine wisdom now be shown by the righteousness with which I speak and act."

December 26. You must hasten to be posted in some science so that you can speak publicly the great thoughts that are nigh your speech. This should be your constant affirmation: "My tongue shall speak of righteousness and of thy praise all the day long."

December 27. How noble are your ideals, sweet friend. They shall all surround your everyday life if you believe this: "The angel of the Lord encampeth round about."

December 28. Money is nothing to you. Therefore, you can have all you like by getting a right thought. Great possessions naturally flow to you if you do not hold a foolish thought strongly. This verse will give you your successful idea: "All my help from Thee I bring."

December 29

Yours is a great and noble nature. Even if some thought has deceived you into misfortune, you may rise speedily into prosperity on these words: "God is my Provider. I am satisfied with the bounty of God."

December 30. Great possibilities of usefulness to the world lie in your nature. You are of the tribe of Judah. Keep this for your life motto: "Good judgment is given unto me."

December 31. Never despise anybody. Think daily that there is no respect of persons with God. Your spiritual nature is your true nobility. This nature showing forth you hold the government of nations in your grasp. This is your text: "Thy vows are upon me,

God; I will render praises unto thee."
END

Made in the USA
Las Vegas, NV
13 January 2022

41330693R00059